Chloé's Curls

Text and illustrations copyright © 2016 by Genté Shaw

Printed in the USA

Paperback ISBN: 978 - 0692832578

10 9 8 7 6 5 4 3 2 1

Sadé Rose Publishing Co.
Portland, OR
SRPublishingCo@gmail.com

I dedicate this book to my
Chloé Christine & Nylá Rose...
You girls have the best of your father and I.
We love you two to the moon and back, again and again!!!

And to every girl with curls...

****

An old wive's tale says "If a pregnant woman has heartburn throughout her pregnancy, the baby will be born with tons of hair."

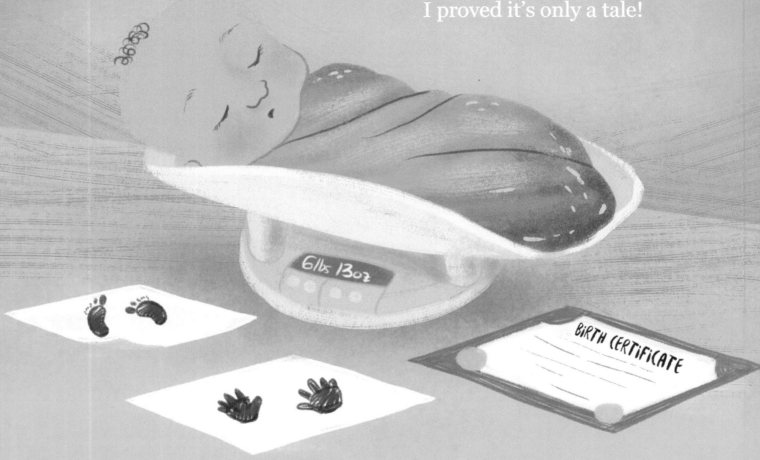

Well.
I proved it's only a tale!

BIRTH CERTIFICATE

6lbs 13oz

Mommy said after all the heartburn she experienced during pregnancy,
I was born with peach fuzz and a single ringlet in the back...

2

..the perfect Shirley Temple curl.

3

And like most babies, the peach fuzz I did have shedded,
leaving my ringlet to adorn the back of my head.

4

Mommy would always dress me in fancy, posh outfits with oversized head bands, hats or bonnets to announce to the world...

SHE'S A GIRL!!!

In fact, the day I turned three months old, Mommy got my ears pierced. She looked forward to the day when she could style my hair with extravagant ribbons and bowrettes.

It wasn't until I was two years old that my hair took off like a rocket ship and began to grow!

7

Every day is an opportunity! There are no limits to where these curls can go!!!

During this time, Mommy nurtured my hair by moisturizing and defining each curl. We trimmed my ends every three months to keep them from splitting.

When I was three years old, my favorite hairstyle was...

The Donut!!!

No, no, no, no…
Not the donut you
eat, but a bun shaped
like a donut.

11

Just another day in my world with these curls!

Now that I am older... I like to wear afro puffs, two strand flat twists, BIG afros with headbands, rope twists with ribbons and cornrows.

LOOKING GOOD!

PERFECT TWISTS!

BEAUTIFUL CUR

YOU ROCK!

During our bedtime stories, Mommy takes her time to loosen my curls. Once my curls are loosened, she adds coconut oil to seal in moisture.
Because my hair is so curly, Mommy has to keep it moisturized otherwise she says, "it will become dry and brittle then it will shed."

I don't want that to happen!!!
After all, it took two years for my hair to grow to this length.

Here's my favorite part... To comfort me, Mommy brushes my scalp which makes falling asleep easy. Then, we pray together as a family.

Now, I'm ready for bed!

Because Mommy brushes my hair the night before, mornings in my world are fashioned with beautifully, bouncy curls.

Either visiting Saturn or taking swimming lessons, these curls know no bounds!!!

From a Mother to Another Mother

After having Chloé, I was overwhelmed with joy then blindsided by fear. As a parent, I am partially yet largely responsible for molding and nurturing another human being. Talk about pressure! I shared these thoughts with my mom through a stream of tears and spasmodic laughter. As always my mom loved on me and said, "Genté, you're not crazy so forget about doing things the 'wrong way'... you are not going to intentionally harm her. And the 'perfect way' does not exist. So find 'you and Chloé's way'." My mom's words of wisdom dispelled fear and encouraged me to be brave.

So here's to being brave!!! Within the next two pages are a few Mommy Notes as to how Chloé and I do things- I wish to share them with you. With time your daughter's hair care regimen may need to change according to her needs... liken to fluid, be flexible.

From one mother to another mother,
Genté Shaw

Mommy's Notes

- For Page 9 -

First moisturize curls with a leave in conditioner, and then add 100% cold pressed Organic Coconut Oil to seal in moisture. This keeps curls defined and lessens the frizz. To aid in further frizz control, use a glycerin product (I use Cantu's Dry Deny). A great way to maintain the length of hair is to trim the ends every three months. This prevents the ends from splitting up the entire hair shaft. (I recommend you have a professional hair designer do this).

- For Page 10 -

A bun shaper can be purchased from your local beauty supply store or drugstore in the hair care section. I made Chloé's from an old shirt sleeve; it's really simple. I cut the sleeve and rolled the sleeve inside of itself in the shape of a donut. Once the sleeve was completely rolled, I covered the bun shaper with a (brand new) brown knee high to camouflage it with Chloe's hair.

- For Page 13 -

Before loosening (detangling) Chloé's curls, I apply coconut oil to her ends then work it up to her roots. Next, I comb small sections of her hair from the ends to her roots to avoid unneccessary breakage. Lastly, I brush her hair from her scalp to the ends. Optional- I like to braid her hair into four three-strand plaits before she goes to bed.

- For Page 14 -

In the mornings, I add a pea size amount of coconut oil to the four plaits to add shine and moisture then I unbraid the plaits, and lastly I style her hair as desired. Generally, I shampoo Chloé's hair once a month with a sulfate-free shampoo (I like Mixed Chicks Kids Shampoo/Conditioner), and I use As I Am's Coconut CoWash to co-wash her hair once a week. In both cases, after rinsing Chloé's hair, I apply a leave in conditioner working it into her hair from ends to roots. This makes combing through her 3b/3c curls from ends to roots with a wide tooth comb very easy. Next, I apply a quarter size amount of SheaMoisture's Curl Enhancing Smoothie to her entire head. Then to seal all of this goodness in, I add coconut oil and Argan oil; again working the products into her hair from ends to roots. At this point, Chloé's curls are completely moisturized and defined. I allow her hair to air dry resulting in beautifully bouncy, curly ringlets.

****

****

CPSIA information can be obtained at www.ICGtesting.com
Printed in the USA
LVIW01n1437250417
532118LV00009B/77

9 780692 832578